Did'

GREAT Y

A MISCELLANY

Compiled by Julia Skinner

With particular reference to the work of Frank Meeres,
Barry Pardue, Neil Storey and Clive Tully

THE FRANCIS FRITH COLLECTION

www.francisfrith.com

First published in the United Kingdom in 2013 by The Francis Frith Collection®

This edition published exclusively for Bradwell Books in 2013
For trade enquiries see: www.bradwellbooks.com or tel: 0800 834 920
ISBN 978-1-84589-724-6

British Library Cataloguing in Publication Data

Did You Know? Great Yarmouth - A Miscellany
Compiled by Julia Skinner
With particular reference to the work of Frank Meeres, Barry Pardue, Neil Storey and Clive Tully

The Francis Frith Collection
6 Oakley Business Park,
Wylye Road, Dinton,
Wiltshire SP3 5EU
Tel: +44 (0) 1722 716 376
Email: info@francisfrith.co.uk
www.francisfrith.com

Printed and bound in Malaysia
Contains material sourced from responsibly managed forests

Front Cover: **GREAT YARMOUTH, REGENT ROAD 1896** 37959p
Frontispiece: **GREAT YARMOUTH, THE AMUSEMENT PARK, BRITANNIA PIER 1908**
60647
Contents: **GREAT YARMOUTH, SCOTTISH FISHING BOATS c1900** G56507

The colour-tinting is for illustrative purposes only, and is not intended to be historically accurate

CONTENTS

INTRODUCTION

The celebrated east coast resort of Great Yarmouth lies at the mouth of the River Yare, and for centuries the town was a flourishing fishing port. In more recent centuries Great Yarmouth has been able to embrace the functions of both port and holiday destination, with its harbour channel to the west and its holiday resort facing east across the North Sea. Begun with a spa and bath-house in the 18th century, the holiday trade in the town developed rapidly from the mid 19th century, when the resort was to become the first Norfolk coastal town to obtain a railway link. Seafront terraces and development grew apace from the 1840s, and soon the Wellington Pier (1854) and Britannia Pier (1858) were stretching their airy promenades out to sea; a tradition of entertainment, innovations, attractions and ornamental gardens was begun in the town.

  Great Yarmouth had its fair share of trials and tribulations in the 20th century. The town was badly bombed during the Second World War when over 200 hundred people were killed, and the damage to the town was significant. Bombing from over 90 air raids caused major destruction, not only to industrial targets but also levelling large sections of the Rows. St Nicholas's Church lost its spire and was completely gutted after being hit by incendiaries in 1942. In 1953 Great Yarmouth suffered along with the rest of the east coast during the worst flooding of the century, when hurricane force winds combined with a high tide allowed the sea to break through numerous sea defences all along the coast. In Great Yarmouth nine people lost their lives, and thousands were evacuated to local holiday camps while the damage was repaired. Sadly, post-war redevelopment of Great Yarmouth was largely unsympathetic, a result of the urgent need for extra housing to replace that lost to the war and slum clearance. The 1950s saw the damage wrought by the war cleared away, and blocks of flats put up in place of the old

Rows houses, while further development in the 1970s established a new road system and town centre. So it was that much of the historic Great Yarmouth was swept away.

In the 1960s a new industry began to take off in the area. The new industrial activity originally started as a search for oil, but whilst there was little to be found, gas was there in abundance. As a result, the port facilities were expanded and improved to service the burgeoning industry. Today, Great Yarmouth has one of the largest offshore marine bases in Europe.

Great Yarmouth – or Yarmouth, as it is known by the locals – remains Norfolk's biggest and most popular coastal resort, but visitors to the town who prefer only to be entertained by the theatres, sideshows and amusements miss a tremendous amount if they fail to look back into the town's history.

GREAT YARMOUTH, THE QUAY 1903 50265

NORFOLK DIALECT
WORDS AND PHRASES

'Afront' – in front.

'Ahind' – behind.

'Atwin' – between.

'Bishy barney bee' – a ladybird.

'Dodman' – a snail.

'Dudder' – to shiver.

'Dwile' – a floor cloth.

'Harnser' – a heron.

'I'll get wrong!' – I'll get told off!

'Lollop' – to move along slowly.

'Luggy' – deaf.

'Lummox' – a clumsy or awkward person.

'Mardle' – to gossip or chat.

'Mavish' – a thrush.

'Mawkin' – a scarecrow.

'Mawther' – a young woman.

'On the huh' – slanted, not level or straight.

'Squit' – talking nonsense.

'Titty-totty' – very small.

'Uhmtie-tump' – a mole hill.

'Warmint' – vermin, or a varmint, a troublesome person.

HAUNTED GREAT YARMOUTH

The ruins of the Roman fort of Burgh Castle near Great Yarmouth (see photograph B498020, page 8) are said to be haunted by the ghosts of people thrown to their deaths from its walls.

There were a number of reported sightings of strange apparitions near the town's now-closed Southtown railway station in January 1860. Some reports described a sort of 'Will 'o the Wisp' apparition, and others described what appeared to be several phantom dogs, one being a large black creature dragging a heavy chain from its neck, and the other being a giant white hound which was also spotted roaming around the marshes near the station, frightening cattle.

The Hippodrome Circus building, on the junction of St Peter's Road and St George's Road, is one of only two surviving custom-built permanent circus buildings in Britain (the other one is in Blackpool), and is said to be haunted by several ghosts. One is the shade of George Gilbert, the famous circus showman who built the Hippodrome in 1903. The other is known as 'Swinging Billy', said to be the ghost of a former circus worker who hanged himself inside the building – for more fascinating information about the ghost stories associated with this building, and eye-witness accounts of the hauntings, see the website www.hippodromememories.com

According to a local legend, if you ran round St George's churchyard three times without stopping and then shouted 'Bloody Queen Mary!', the face of Queen Mary I would appear at the nearest window of the church. The reason for this is now forgotten, and seems especially odd since the custom referred to the unpopular Queen Mary who lived in Tudor times, and St George's Church was built in the early 18th century.

GREAT YARMOUTH, KING STREET 1896 37957

GREAT YARMOUTH MISCELLANY

Although the earliest reference to Great Yarmouth is in the Domesday Book of 1086, the town's origins are much older. It was back in Roman times, when the forts of Caister (north of Great Yarmouth) and Burgh Castle (to the south-west, now inland) stood on the estuary of a large river, that a large sandbank began to build up. It was a wild and windy place, and the reason the first settlers came here – undoubtedly fishermen – was because the sea was absolutely alive with fish. As the settlement grew, what started as just a small gathering of fishermen grew into a thriving port.

Great Yarmouth gained the first of its 25 charters in 1208, granted by King John. Just over 50 years later, Henry III gave the town permission to build a town wall and moat, to protect the three sides which were not backing on to the river. Over a mile long, twenty-three feet high and seven feet thick, and with ten gates to provide access into the town, the wall was to turn Great Yarmouth into something of a fortress, although lack of money and the ravages of the plague meant it was not completed until the reign of Edward III in the 14th century. When the town wall was finished, it also included many defensive towers like the North Tower seen in the photograph on the opposite page.

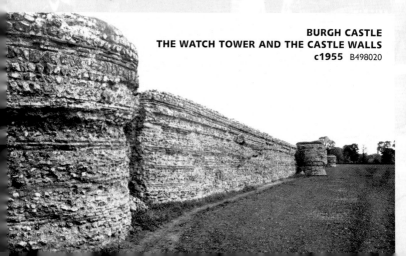

BURGH CASTLE
THE WATCH TOWER AND THE CASTLE WALLS
c1955 B498020

GREAT YARMOUTH
NORTH TOWER
1891 28708

This photograph shows the Blackfriars Tower, one of a number of towers built with the defensive walls of the town between 1284 and 1396. It was raised in height during the 16th century, at the time of the threat of the Spanish Armada, and the stretch of wall near the Blackfriars Tower was repaired using a combination of local flint and limestone from the nearby monastery of the Black Friars (of the Dominican order), which had burnt down in 1522. The Blackfriars Tower, otherwise known as the south-east tower, was used in the 19th century as a shop at street level with accommodation above – there was even a small cottage built on top. Today the modern additions have been removed, and the town wall and tower are revealed and restored.

In medieval times there was a castle at the centre of the walled town as well, but it only survived until 1621, when it was ordered to be demolished.

**GREAT YARMOUTH
BLACKFRIARS TOWER
1908** 60653

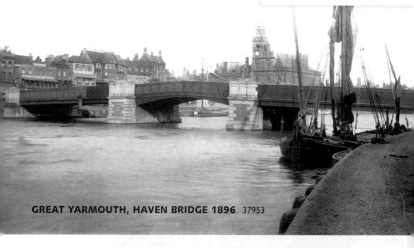

GREAT YARMOUTH, HAVEN BRIDGE 1896 37953

Up to the middle of the 14th century, all but the smallest of ships were unable to sail into the harbour, or haven; they had to unload at sea, anchored in Yarmouth Roads, the navigable stretch between the coast and sandbanks offshore. The longshore drift which produced the sandbank on which Great Yarmouth is built is a constant action, and as the flow out of the river mouth was not strong enough to scour it out, it continually choked up with sand and shingle. In 1347 a new outlet for the river was created closer to the town to provide an entrance to the harbour. It was a failure, and the next two hundred years saw successive attempts to create harbour entrances which would not silt up, each at different locations. The seventh attempt in 1560 saw a Dutch expert brought in at great expense to supervise the building of a new cut, this time stabilised by wooden piling. It worked, and it survives to this day as Great Yarmouth's harbour entrance.

Haven Bridge joins Great Yarmouth with Southtown. The centre section lifts up to allow the passage of boats. The bridge seen in this view taken in 1896 was replaced in 1930.

GREAT YARMOUTH, THE TOWN HALL 1922 72535

Along Great Yarmouth's South Quay there are a few old flint-faced
buildings, but many of the buildings show a strong Continental
appearance, especially reminiscent of Amsterdam. Even Charles
Dickens's character David Copperfield in his novel of that name
noticed the Dutch influence; like Holland, Great Yarmouth was
taken back from the sea, which periodically tries to take it back by
disastrous flooding. In the 18th century, Dutch and Great Yarmouth
fishermen were extremely friendly, and at one time 'Dutch Sunday'
(the first Sunday before 21st September) was observed in the town
with a ceremony called 'wetting the nets', which people came from
all over Norfolk to see. Dutch and local dignitaries wore their most
flamboyant uniforms and robes, and the townsfolk and visitors wore
their Sunday best clothes.

The quay at Great Yarmouth was described by Daniel Defoe in 1724 as 'the finest quay in England, if not Europe'. It would be hard to disagree, for the town's broad quays are up to 150 yards wide in places, and are lined with magnificent merchants' houses. To the right of photograph 60652 (below) is the original Star Hotel, which was formerly the home of William Crowe, a member of the Company of Spanish Merchants which conducted trade with the Netherlands, and bailiff of Great Yarmouth in 1594 and 1606; its rich ornamentation was designed to display Crowe's enormous wealth. The Star Hotel later moved north, and now occupies the building which was called the Cromwell Hotel in this 1908 photograph, second from the right. The old Star Hotel building seen in this photograph was demolished to make way for the telephone exchange; it contained beautiful panelling, which is now in the Metropolitan Museum of Art in New York in the United States of America.

GREAT YARMOUTH, HALL QUAY 1908 60652

Huddled around the quay in the past were the town's famous and unique Rows, 156 parallel narrow alleyways which ran from east to west between the Market Place and King Street on one side, and the Quays along the river on the other. The Rows developed in this way in medieval times, as a result of houses having to be crammed close together within the perimeter of the town walls. The Rows were likened by the 19th-century author Charles Dickens to the bars of a grid-iron. Congested with cottages, whitewashed yards and washing lines, they were the home ground of the working population of the town. The Rows all had names, many of them taken from nearby inns; some names were picturesque, like Kitty Witches Row. They were also given numbers in 1804 to avoid confusion. Most of the Rows were severely damaged by enemy bombing during the Second World War.

Passageways between the blocks of houses in the Rows could be as narrow as 30 inches, and special carts called 'trolls' were developed to negotiate the wider alleyways; 12 feet long and 3½ feet across, their wheels were set beneath the body of the cart rather than the outside – nowadays there is a modern replica of a troll on display outside Great Yarmouth's Town Hall.

By today's standards, Great Yarmouth's Rows were dark, dingy and overcrowded, with crude sanitation, but despite these bad conditions there was very little sickness there, which was attributed to the constant draught of air along the narrow passages. Indeed, there are records of numerous cases of longevity amongst the residents of the Rows, including Matthew Champion, who died in 1793 aged 111, and Luke Waller, who died in 1824 at the age of 105!

GREAT YARMOUTH
A MISCELLANY

GREAT YARMOUTH, ROW NUMBER 60 1908   60654

Although the port of Great Yarmouth had a prosperous general trade, the town's prosperity was founded on herring fishing. In medieval Europe, herring was an important foodstuff – it was nutritious, and it kept well if smoked – and was supplied to everyone from peasants to nobility. From Great Yarmouth, the fish was exported to all over Europe, and by the middle of the 13th century the town was booming. The first forty-day-long Great Yarmouth Herring Fair was held in 1270, and continued to be held every year for another five hundred years.

In the Middle Ages the Confederation of the Cinque Ports was a group of medieval ports, all but one in Kent and East Sussex, which in return for considerable rights and privileges provided the monarch with vessels and mariners for ship service, thus forming an important naval force of the Middle Ages. Included in the privileges enjoyed by the Cinque Portsmen were the rights of 'Den and Strand', which allowed fishermen from the Cinque Ports to land their boats at what is now Great Yarmouth in the herring season without paying a fee, to sell their catch without charge, and to dry and mend their nets on the shore. Fishermen from the Cinque Ports had been making an annual visit to the herring fishing grounds off the East Anglian coast for hundreds of years but their problem was to land their catch and get it to market before it went off, so these rights were extremely valuable. The rights of Den and Strand also entitled the Portsmen to run Great Yarmouth's important annual Herring Fair. The control by Cinque Ports' bailiffs of the lucrative administration and policing of the Fair was bitterly resented in the town, but the privilege continued until it was abolished by King Charles II in the 17th century – a long chapter in the Confederation's history came to an end in 1663 with the last official visit of the Cinque Ports' bailiffs to Great Yarmouth to take charge of the Herring Fair.

From the Middle Ages onwards there were many smokehouses in Great Yarmouth where herrings were turned into 'red herrings' (salted herrings that were smoked for up to 6 weeks until they were hard and dry – originally to ensure a long preservation in medieval times), kippers, buckling (herring hot-smoked with the guts and roe left in) and the famous Yarmouth bloaters for which the town was renowned. A bloater is a whole ungutted herring that is not split open down the back, like a kipper, before being lightly smoked for up to 12 hours – they are delicious, with a slightly gamey flavour. They should be eaten straight after coming from the smoker, and certainly within 48 hours, and are best served either as they are bought fresh, without further cooking, or simply grilled with butter and eaten with bread and butter. These traditional products are still made in Great Yarmouth by HS Fishing 2000 Ltd at the Smoke House at Sutton Road, South Denes.

Great Yarmouth's fishing industry reached its height in the 19th century, thanks to better-equipped boats and the arrival of the railways, which ensured more efficient distribution to markets, and by the end of the 19th century Great Yarmouth was the leading herring port in the world. During the herring season, which lasted about ten weeks from the end of September, the town's population would be swelled by thousands of fishermen with their wives and daughters who gutted and packed the fish – this was a skilled job, and a good herring woman could gut 40 fish a minute. Herrings were also dried and cured into the famous Yarmouth bloaters. The late 19th century saw a huge impact on Great Yarmouth's fishing industry with the annual migration of hundreds of fishing boats from Scotland arriving for the autumn fishing season. The Scottish fishermen and their wives and daughters brought with them a method for pickling the fish in brine, rather than the traditional method of smoking which produced the Yarmouth bloater, and pickled herring had overtaken smoked herring in popularity by the turn of the 19th and 20th centuries.

GREAT YARMOUTH, THE FISH MARKET c1900 G56503

This photograph shows Great Yarmouth's fish market around 1900. After a good fishing trip, the drifters have unloaded their haul into baskets known as 'swills', specially-made wicker baskets for herrings which were unique to Great Yarmouth and Lowestoft. Here on the wharf the tellers (in bowler hats) would assess the catch prior to its sale by auction. Great Yarmouth's herring fishing industry continued up to the second half of the 20th century, although sailing boats were superseded by steam drifters, but by the 1950s it was clear that fish stocks were depleted, and the herring industry eventually came to an end. By the time they were sold in the early 1960s, Great Yarmouth's fleet of fishing boats had dwindled to just six vessels. Great Yarmouth's once-mighty herring fleet is now gone, but the town's fishing heritage is commemorated in the excellent Time and Tide Museum on Blackfriar's Road, housed in a former herring smokery.

An interesting blend of the old and the new can be seen in this photograph of Great Yarmouth's harbour around 1900. The boats in the foreground are sail, while further back are some steam drifters. At times the harbour would be so jam-packed that it would be possible to cross from Great Yarmouth to Southtown on the other side of the river simply by climbing from one boat to another.

Although Great Yarmouth made its name on herring fishery, it was also a great centre of ship-building, which also made it a significant naval port. By the 14th century Great Yarmouth had its own navy comprising 20 men-of-war, which was more fire-power than could be mustered even by London at that time.

GREAT YARMOUTH, THE HARBOUR c1900 G56510

Great Yarmouth's imposing Grade II listed Town Hall is one of the most beautiful buildings in the town. It was built in the early 1880s and is a fine example of Victorian Gothic style, designed by the architect John B Pearce. The Town Hall houses a wealth of history about the town from engraved records of the early bailiffs (the forerunners of councillors) to displays of mayoral regalia, historical maps and portraits. Also in the Town Hall is the town's 'Hutch', a brightly painted wooden chest made of wood with wrought iron keys and bolts which was used in the past as a place of safekeeping for the ancient records of the town council.

GREAT YARMOUTH, THE TOWN HALL 1893 33382

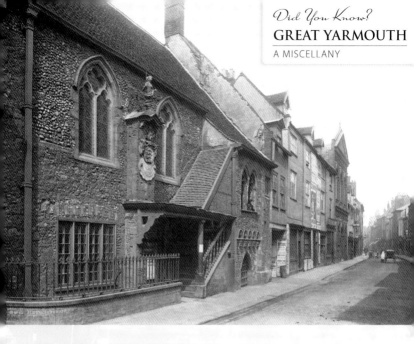

GREAT YARMOUTH, THE FREE LIBRARY (THE TOLHOUSE) 1891
28703

This photograph shows the historic Tolhouse, which at the time this view was taken was being used as the town's free library. Before its restoration in 1883 the impressive flint-built Tolhouse had been home to the police. It was built in the 13th century, and it served as Great Yarmouth's town hall, court and gaol for 600 hundred years – the Tolhouse is the oldest surviving civic building in England. In 1645 the Corporation of Great Yarmouth sent for Matthew Hopkins, James I's infamous Witchfinder General, to investigate sixteen local women accused of being witches; five of the women were condemned to death, and they were held in the dungeon of the Tolhouse before their execution – the grated window at street level is the dungeon window. The Tolhouse is now used as a museum.

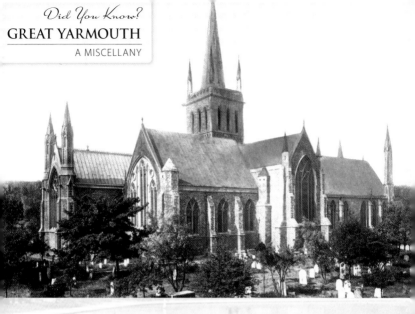

**GREAT YARMOUTH, ST NICHOLAS'S CHURCH FROM THE
NORTH-EAST 1890** 37962

The glory of Great Yarmouth is its parish church of St Nicholas.
Originally a simple Norman construction of 1101, over the years it
expanded with the town. The initial cruciform shape was filled out
to make a rectangular shape, eventually fulfilling a claim to be the
largest parish church in England. St Nicholas's Church is seen in all
its glory, complete with its spire, in this photograph of 1890. Prior
to 1803, the spire of the church appeared crooked whichever way
it was viewed, and as it was considered insecure it was taken down
and replaced with a new spire 168ft high which was covered in sheet
copper. The spire was used as a landmark for passing ships for many
years, most appropriate for a church dedicated to St Nicholas, the
patron saint of mariners. The church was badly damaged by bombing
in 1942, during the Second World War, and when it was rebuilt it was
given a neo-Gothic interior with broad aisles. Unfortunately the funds
for the church's rebuilding could not stretch to a replacement spire,
so photographs of the church with its spire, such as 19896 (opposite)
and 72526 (pages 38-39), show one of the town's now-vanished views.

There are few very old buildings surviving in Great Yarmouth, but the town still has the fishermen's almshouses, or Hospital, and the Tolhouse, the oldest municipal building in England (seen in photograph 28703 on page 21). The Fishermen's Hospital is shown in this photograph. The hospital was founded in 1702; it could accommodate up to twenty former fishermen, who were either disabled or over 60 years old, and their wives. However, if a fisherman died, his widow had to leave the hospital – unless she could persuade one of the other fishermen there to marry her! The Fishermen's Hospital is a series of 20 small cottages, each with one room downstairs and a bedroom built into the roof. In the background of this photograph is the now-lost spire of St Nicholas's Church.

GREAT YARMOUTH, THE FISHERMEN'S HOSPITAL 1887 19896

Halfway along King Street is St George's Church, one of the few Classical-style churches in East Anglia. It was built in 1714 by John Price, modelled on a baroque design borrowed from Christopher Wren, and endowed by a special Act of Parliament. This historic church has characteristic 18th-century galleries, pulpit and reredos, and a plaster ceiling above the nave. St George's Church is now used as an arts centre.

The 19th-century writer George Borrow lived in King Street, in a house close to St George's Church, between 1835 and 1855. He wrote a number of novels and travelogues based on his own journeys around both Britain and Europe, but is particularly remembered for his works 'Lavengro' (1851) and 'The Romany Rye' (1857), which record the time he spent with Romani (Gypsy) people in Britain.

GREAT YARMOUTH, ST GEORGE'S CHURCH 1891 28723

GREAT YARMOUTH, REGENT ROAD 1896 37959

This photograph shows a peaceful scene of Regent Road, well away
from the bustle of the seafront. In the hazy distance are the sails
of boats. The street is lined with a medley of newly-constructed
buildings. Victorian Great Yarmouth grew out of the efforts of
individual speculators, with the consequence that there was no
prevailing plan or blueprint to ensure a harmonious townscape, as
there would have been in Georgian times. Along the road on the
left is where Docwra's famous rock-making factory was established.
One of the youths posing for the photographer is holding a goat
harnessed to a small cart, which would have been used for giving
children rides on the beach. Goat carriages were a characteristic form
of children's amusement in 19th-century Great Yarmouth, but animal
lovers objected to them, and they were banned by the Borough
Council in 1911 – although the goat in this photograph looks happy
enough.

The photograph below shows the former St Peter's Church on St Peter's Road. Dating back to the 1830s, St Peter's claim to fame is that it was the first church in England to suffer bomb damage during the First World War. When St Nicholas's Church was bombed during the Second World War, St Peter's took over its role. The building was subsequently taken over for use by the Greek Orthodox Church, and is now known as St Spiridon's Greek Orthodox Church.

Photograph 28724 on the opposite page, top, shows the Roman Catholic Church of St Mary in Regent Road, which was built in the perpendicular style in 1850. Previously, Catholics had assembled for worship in a room in Howard Street. Photograph 37972 on the opposite page, bottom, shows St George's Park, which opened in 1866. The large building on the right of the photograph is Park Baptist Church; next door the Men's Room ran Sunday afternoon Bible classes for men of all ages. During the evenings, recreational activities such as billiards and dominoes would be available. The church was demolished in 1990 and a new one built.

GREAT YARMOUTH, ST PETER'S CHURCH 1896 37969

**GREAT YARMOUTH, THE ROMAN CATHOLIC CHURCH
REGENT ROAD 1891** 28724

GREAT YARMOUTH, ST GEORGE'S PARK 1896 37972

GREAT YARMOUTH, THE BEACH 1887 19860

Norfolk began to attract tourists in a small way when sea-bathing
became fashionable in the mid 18th century, and Great Yarmouth's
popularity as a holiday resort goes back to 1759, when its first Bath
House was opened on the seafront. Seawater was pumped up to two
small baths, one for men and one for women. At this time fashionable
people both drank salt water and bathed in it as a 'cure-all'. Ladies
who came to bathe in the sea demanded modesty – thus the bathing
hut was invented, a changing-room on wheels which was dragged
down to the water's edge by a horse, with steps down from which
the bather could enter the water, and there were bathing machines
on the beach at Great Yarmouth as early as 1819. Great Yarmouth
began to develop seriously as a resort in the 1840s with the arrival
of the railway, which brought large numbers of visitors from the
industrial midlands and the north to enjoy the miles of beautiful
sandy beaches.

The first railway in Norfolk ran from Great Yarmouth to Norwich, opening in 1844. The coming of the railways had a dramatic impact on the town. Communications with the Midlands and London were soon opened up when the line between Norwich and Cambridge opened in 1845. The line was extended from the main station to South Quay as early as 1847, and ran all the way down the Quay to the Fish Wharf by 1882. This line was for freight traffic only, and was used to carry fish, and also to supply coal to steam drifters moored against the Quay. The line closed down in 1976. Other lines followed, connecting Great Yarmouth (Southtown) with London via Ipswich and also via Lowestoft. A third station in the town, Yarmouth Beach, supplied a connection to the Midlands and the North.

GREAT YARMOUTH, THE BATHING POOL AND JETTY c1955 G56041

GREAT YARMOUTH, THE BEACH c1900 G56505

Did You Know?
GREAT YARMOUTH
A MISCELLANY

GREAT YARMOUTH, THE REVOLVING TOWER 1922 72518

Always Norfolk's biggest and most popular holiday resort, Great Yarmouth constantly sought to find the latest attraction. It was known for its pleasure beach, and before the days of the scenic railway visitors could get a bird's eye view of the town from the Revolving Tower, seen in this photograph. Built in 1897, it was 120ft high with a cage capable of holding 150 people that rotated as it went up and down. It was just one of five in the whole country. The tower was demolished in 1941 and the metal from it was sent for wartime salvage.

The Royal Aquarium was built as a leisure complex, housing a skating rink, aquarium, bars and restaurants. A huge budget of £50,000 was provided for the building, but only half was used, and it was never completed. The venue was unsuccessful as an aquarium and the building was then converted into a theatre which hosted everything from West End plays to musicals, earning its Royal prefix after gaining the patronage of Edward, Prince of Wales (later Edward VII). Today the building is used as a cinema. The façade is constructed in gault brick from Costessey, a village just outside Norwich.

GREAT YARMOUTH, THE ROYAL AQUARIUM 1895 37951

GREAT YARMOUTH, WELLINGTON PIER AND THE WINTER GARDEN c1955 G56036

Many seaside piers began life as landing stages for pleasure steamers. Thrusting out into the sea, they encapsulated the Victorian passion for exotic feats of engineering. Piers were soon the focus for holiday fun, where visitors could enjoy a concert, promenade or simply sit, watching the crowds flow by. Wellington Pier at Great Yarmouth opened in 1854. It was acquired by the Corporation in 1900, and they rebuilt the pier with a pavilion and promenade in 1903. In 1904 they purchased the glass Winter Garden at Torquay in Devon at a knockdown price, dismantled it, brought it to Great Yarmouth by barge (without a single pane of glass being broken) and re-erected it beside the pier entrance.

Originally built in 1858 for £6,000, the Britannia Pier at Great Yarmouth was rebuilt in 1901-02 with a new pavilion built by the Norwich company Boulton & Paul – it is seen newly built in the photograph on the opposite page. In December 1909 the pavilion burnt down, but a replacement was soon erected to seat 1,400 people.

GREAT YARMOUTH, THE WINTER GARDEN 1908 60650

GREAT YARMOUTH, BRITANNIA PIER 1904 52337

The large, imposing building seen in this photograph was originally The Gem, the first cinema in Norfolk, and one of the first buildings erected in the country for the sole purpose of showing films. In its early years the authorities insisted that men and women sit in separate parts of the auditorium. It became the Windmill Theatre in 1946; its first show featured the up-and-coming comedian Norman Wisdom.

GREAT YARMOUTH, THE WINDMILL THEATRE c1955 G56030

GREAT YARMOUTH, THE WATERWAYS c1960 G56071

The Venetian Waterways were laid out in the 1920s as an exercise to help provide work for some of the town's unemployed, during the Great Depression. At that date, the boats were not embellished with large brightly coloured fish, as seen in this 1960s' photograph.

GREAT YARMOUTH, THE MARKET
1922 72526

GREAT YARMOUTH, THE MARKET PLACE 1908 60651

Great Yarmouth's market has been the heart of the town for at least 800 years. In the 20th and 21st centuries it has become famous for the high quality of the chips sold on its stalls, and the market stalls seen in the photograph of the market in 1922 on the previous pages include Brewer's Chip Potato Saloon in the centre, by the lamp post. Electric trams are also seen in that photograph, as well as the view of the market place on this page. A ride on a tram was a key memory of many Great Yarmouth holidaymakers in the past. Horse-drawn trams operated in the last decades of the 19th century. Electric trams began to operate in 1902 – the fare was just one penny. In 1922 four million passengers a year were being carried on the trams, at an average fare of just over two pence a ride. Trams ran along the seafront between Wellington Pier and Britannia Pier, and connected the front with the Market Place and Vauxhall railway station, which was reached by a bridge shared by the railway. The trams began to be replaced with buses in the late 1920s, and the last tram between Great Yarmouth and Gorleston ran on 25th September 1930.

In the 18th and early 19th centuries the English naval fleet often gathered in the Yarmouth Roads before sailing to engage the enemy. The great naval hero Vice-Admiral Lord Nelson, a Norfolk man (born in Burnham Thorpe in 1758), frequently embarked and landed at Great Yarmouth, including two triumphant landings after his victories at the Battles of the Nile (1798) and Copenhagen (1801). When Nelson landed at Gorleston in 1800 he received a hero's welcome and was escorted to the Wrestlers' Arms in Great Yarmouth and presented with the Freedom of the Borough. A local legend is that the landlady of the inn asked if she could rename her establishment the Nelson Arms in his honour. 'That', Nelson replied, 'would be ridiculous, seeing as I have but one'. Nelson had, of course, lost an arm at the Battle of Santa Cruz de Tenerife in 1797.

As with many towns and cities, Great Yarmouth has more than a smattering of streets and terraces named after Britain's great military heroes – Wellington, Kitchener and Nelson. But with Vice-Admiral Lord Nelson's links with Great Yarmouth one might, quite rightly, expect a little more, which is why a road, a court, a terrace and even a square in the town are named after Nelson's most famous battle, at Trafalgar in 1805. Nowadays, Great Yarmouth celebrates the life and achievements of Lord Nelson in the Norfolk Nelson Museum on South Quay. The museum holds a large collection of his letters, keepsakes, paintings, and medals, as well as a recreation of his study from his home in Surrey, complete with a wax model of Lord Nelson at his desk. A replica of a ship from Nelson's time shows what it was like to be a sailor in his navy, with an interactive display. Children can climb into hammocks, hear commands shouted out amidst the commotion of a naval battle during the Napoleonic Wars, and experience the sights and smells of life on board a warship.

After Lord Nelson's death at the Battle of Trafalgar in 1805, Great Yarmouth was chosen as the most fitting place for a Norfolk memorial to him, sited on the coast in the South Denes – now surrounded by industrial units. Designed by Norfolk-born architect William Wilkins, the 144ft-tall monument was erected in 1819, 24 years after the taller and better-known column which stands in London's Trafalgar Square. It is usually known as the Nelson Monument, but its correct name is the Norfolk Naval Pillar, although it has also been called the Britannia Monument, after the figure of Britannia which stands on the top. A local legend about the Nelson Monument is that the architect jumped to his death from the top in despair when he realised that the figure of Britannia which tops the monument was facing the 'wrong' way, looking inland rather than out to sea. In fact, it is generally believed that Britannia was designed to look in this direction because she is looking towards Burnham Thorpe, Nelson's birthplace on the north Norfolk coast near King's Lynn.

Inside the Nelson Monument is a spiral staircase leading up to a viewing platform right at the top of the column. From here, there are glorious views out to sea and over the Norfolk countryside – it is said that on a fine day you can see the sun sparkle on the Norfolk Broads. The monument was closed to visitors for many years for safety reasons, but has now been completely repaired and restored; it is opened to the public on limited occasions so that visitors can once again enjoy the views from its summit, as was originally intended. Information about the opening dates and the guided tours of the monument can be obtained from the Norfolk Nelson Museum on South Quay.

Great Yarmouth occupies a spit of land which deflects the River
Yare from entering the sea for three miles. South of the main resort,
not far from the harbour entrance, is South Denes, now given
over to caravan sites. It was an undeveloped sandy heath until
the Napoleonic Wars, when a military garrison was based there.
The barrack master was Captain George Manby, who invented the
breeches buoy and many other nautical life-saving devices. Sailing
drifters are shown moored on the River Yare in this photograph. The
opposite bank in this photograph is South Denes, where an early
tented holiday camp has been erected on the race course. It was only
after the Second World War that caravans replaced tents. Today all
this land is covered with industrial buildings.

GREAT YARMOUTH, THE RIVER YARE c1900 G56506

SPORTING GREAT YARMOUTH

Yarmouth has an important horse-racing course and the annual Eastern Festival of racing is a highlight in the local calendar, with 3 days of flat racing. The first racecourse at Great Yarmouth was built on the Denes in 1810, so that officers from the military barracks there could race and exercise their horses. The current racecourse at Jellicoe Road was established in 1921. It is a popular course with high quality racing, attracting the top trainers and jockeys. In recent years the facilities at the racecourse have been improved and developed at some expense, and the new Lord Nelson Grandstand was opened in 2004.

Great Yarmouth Town Football Club was established in 1897, and was one of the founder members of the Eastern Counties League in 1935. The club's nickname is 'The Bloaters', after the famous Yarmouth bloaters produced in the town. One of the club's most impressive seasons was 1926-27 – despite losing the first league game of the season, they went on to be undefeated in the remaining 23 games that year. Perhaps the club's finest hour was in the FA Cup tournament of the 1953-54 season when they pulled off one of the famous 'giant-killing' acts for which the FA Cup is famous, defeating Crystal Palace to reach the second round of the tournament.

Speedway racing was popular in Great Yarmouth from 1948 to 1962, staged in the greyhound racing stadium in Caister Road. Like the football club, the speedway team was also known as the Yarmouth Bloaters after the smoked fish that Yarmouth is famous for, and the riders wore a emblem of a silver fish on their race jackets.

A modern addition to Great Yarmouth's sporting facilities came in 2008, when the world's first Segway Grand Prix track was opened at the Pleasure Beach gardens. A Segway is a two-wheeled electric vehicle on which the rider balances as the vehicle moves along. The vehicle is steered by the rider leaning forward, backwards, and left or right, whilst using a tall steering handlebar.

GREAT YARMOUTH, REGENT ROAD
c1955   G56039

Did You Know?

GREAT YARMOUTH

A MISCELLANY

QUIZ QUESTIONS

Answers on page 50.

1. One of Great Yarmouth's famous Rows was given the intriguing name of Snatchbody Row – why was this?

2. Which Great Yarmouth MP put his name to an historic document that cost him his life?

3. Which author of a famous children's book was born in Great Yarmouth in 1820?

4. Great Yarmouth had the misfortune to be one of the first places in Britain to suffer what in 1915?

5. Just off the end of the Market Place on Church Plain is the Fishermen's Hospital, founded in 1702. Its archway is topped by a cupola which houses a painted statue … of who?

6. What did the slang phrase 'Going to Yarmouth' mean to sailors in the past?

7. When did Yarmouth become 'Great'?

8. Who was the king commemorated in the name of King Street?

9. On each side of the base of the Nelson Monument at South Denes are carved the names of the ships in which Vice-Admiral Lord Nelson achieved his most famous naval victories: the Captain, the Elephant, the Vanguard and finally the Victory. Above these names are carved the names of the naval battles in which they were engaged – can you name them?

10. Which literary character declared that 'it was well known that Yarmouth was, upon the whole, the finest place in the universe'?

GREAT YARMOUTH, KING STREET 1896 37957x

RECIPE

SOUSED HERRINGS

4 herrings, filleted
25g/1oz plain flour
Half a teaspoonful of powdered mace
25g/1oz butter
Salt and pepper
1 teaspoonful of chopped fresh parsley
1 bay leaf
150ml/ ¼ pint water
150ml/ ¼ pint malt vinegar

Pre-heat the oven to 190°C/375°F/Gas Mark 5.

Mix the flour with the salt, pepper and mace, and use it to dust the herring fillets. Place a small knob of butter in the centre of each fillet, sprinkle the fillet with chopped parsley and roll it up, skin side out. Secure each herring roll with a wooden cocktail stick.

Place the herrings in an ovenproof dish, and add the water, vinegar and bay leaf. Cover the dish and bake for 1 hour in the pre-heated oven.

Remove from the oven and leave the herrings to cool completely in the cooking liquid before serving. Eat cold, served with slices of bread and butter.

RECIPE

Yarmouth Biscuits

350g/12oz plain flour
175g/6oz currants
225g/8oz butter, softened to room temperature
225g/8oz caster sugar
3 eggs, beaten

Pre-heat the oven to 190°C/375°F/Gas Mark 5. Grease two baking
sheets. Thoroughly mix together the currants, butter, sugar, flour
and beaten eggs to make a thick paste and knead lightly. Roll out
the dough on a lightly floured surface and cut it into rounds with a
biscuit cutter. Place the rounds on the greased baking sheets and
bake in the pre-heated oven for 15-20 minutes, until the biscuits
are golden brown.

GREAT YARMOUTH, THE JETTY 1908 60648

QUIZ ANSWERS

1. Snatchbody Row (Row 6) was named after the body-snatcher Thomas Vaughan who lived here in the 19th century. Vaughan rented a room in a house in Row 6, where he kept bodies he had dug out of St Nicholas's churchyard shortly after they had been buried, until he could send them to London, where he sold the bodies to anatomy students (who at that time had no other way of obtaining bodies for anatomy and dissection research). He is believed to have sold at least 10 bodies in this way.

2. The Great Yarmouth MP Miles Corbet supported the Parliamentarian cause during the Civil War, and such was his allegiance and friendship with Oliver Cromwell that he was one of the signatories to Charles I's death warrant in 1649. After the king's son was restored to the throne in 1660 as Charles II, Miles Corbet fled to Holland, but he was arrested and brought back to stand trial. He was condemned to death for high treason, and suffered the ghastly death of being hanged, drawn and quartered.

3. Anna Sewell, the author of the classic children's book 'Black Beauty', was born into a Great Yarmouth Quaker family in 1820 in a delightful timbered house on Church Plain, near St Nicholas's Church, which still survives to this day. In 1834, when she was 14, Anna slipped and twisted her ankle; it never healed and she was ill for the rest of her life. She wrote just one book, and that not until she was 57 years old. 'Black Beauty', published in 1877, sold over a million copies in the next 15 years, and has sold at least 40 million copies since. It was written to protest against cruelty to horses, and the book did its job: animal welfare campaigners gave free copies to stable-hands and cab-drivers. Anna knew she would not live to see its success, as she started writing it after her doctor had given her 18 months to live, and she died just four months after the book was published. She would not have shared in the success of the book financially anyway: her mother sold the copyright to Jarrold's for a mere £20!

4. Although a great number of British towns suffered air raids during the Second World War, only a few places had the misfortune to experience air raids in the First World War, and Great Yarmouth was among them. Great Yarmouth and King's Lynn, both in Norfolk, were the first towns to be attacked by a German Zeppelin airship during the war, when they suffered an aerial bombardment in January 1915.

5. The cupola on the archway of the Fishermen's Hospital houses a painted statue of St Peter – the patron saint of fishermen.

6. In 1809, during the Napoleonic Wars, a Royal Naval Hospital was built on the Denes for wounded sailers. The building was later incorporated into the Militia Barracks, but forty years later it was converted back into a hospital once more, where sailors who were mentally ill were sent for treatment. Thus the phrase 'Going to Yarmouth' became naval slang for someone showing signs of mental strain.

7. The earliest known document to call the town Great Yarmouth comes from the reign of Edward I (1272-1307). It was called Great Yarmouth to distinguish it from Little Yarmouth on the other side of the river, now known as Southtown, and not to distinguish it (as many people think) from Yarmouth on the Isle of Wight.

8. King Street is named after Charles II, who visited Great Yarmouth in 1671.

9. The naval battles in which Nelson achieved victories in the ships depicted on the Nelson Monument were Cape St Vincent (1797), Copenhagen (1801), the Nile, or Aboukir Bay (1798), and Trafalgar (1805).

10. Ham Peggotty, in 'David Copperfield' by Charles Dickens. Dickens came to Great Yarmouth whilst he was writing David Copperfield and the character of Peggotty is believed to have been partly based on a local man he met on his visit, James Sharman, who was the first custodian of the Britannia Monument (Nelson Monument). Sharman was press-ganged into the navy at the age of 14, and later served on the 'Victory' at the Battle of Trafalgar in 1805.

GREAT YARMOUTH, KING STREET
1896 37958

52

FRANCIS FRITH

PIONEER   VICTORIAN   PHOTOGRAPHER

Francis Frith, founder of the world-famous photographic archive, was a complex and multi-talented man. A devout Quaker and a highly successful Victorian businessman, he was philosophical by nature and pioneering in outlook. By 1855 he had already established a wholesale grocery business in Liverpool, and sold it for the astonishing sum of £200,000, which is the equivalent today of over £15,000,000. Now in his thirties, and captivated by the new science of photography, Frith set out on a series of pioneering journeys up the Nile and to the Near East.

INTRIGUE AND EXPLORATION

He was the first photographer to venture beyond the sixth cataract of the Nile. Africa was still the mysterious 'Dark Continent', and Stanley and Livingstone's historic meeting was a decade into the future. The conditions for picture taking confound belief. He laboured for hours in his wicker dark-room in the sweltering heat of the desert, while the volatile chemicals fizzed dangerously in their trays. Back in London he exhibited his photographs and was 'rapturously cheered' by members of the Royal Society. His reputation as a photographer was made overnight.

VENTURE OF A LIFE-TIME

By the 1870s the railways had threaded their way across the country, and Bank Holidays and half-day Saturdays had been made obligatory by Act of Parliament. All of a sudden the working man and his family were able to enjoy days out, take holidays, and see a little more of the world.

With typical business acumen, Francis Frith foresaw that these new tourists would enjoy having souvenirs to commemorate their days out. For the next thirty years he travelled the country by train and by pony and trap, producing fine photographs of seaside resorts and beauty spots that were keenly bought by millions of Victorians. These prints were painstakingly pasted into family albums and pored over during the dark nights of winter, rekindling precious memories of summer excursions. Frith's studio was soon supplying retail shops all over the country, and by 1890 F Frith & Co had become the greatest specialist photographic publishing company in the world, with over 2,000 sales outlets, and pioneered the picture postcard.

FRANCIS FRITH'S LEGACY

Francis Frith had died in 1898 at his villa in Cannes, his great project still growing. By 1970 the archive he created contained over a third of a million pictures showing 7,000 British towns and villages.

Frith's legacy to us today is of immense significance and value, for the magnificent archive of evocative photographs he created provides a unique record of change in the cities, towns and villages throughout Britain over a century and more. Frith and his fellow studio photographers revisited locations many times down the years to update their views, compiling for us an enthralling and colourful pageant of British life and character.

We are fortunate that Frith was dedicated to recording the minutiae of everyday life. For it is this sheer wealth of visual data, the painstaking chronicle of changes in dress, transport, street layouts, buildings, housing and landscape that captivates us so much today, offering us a powerful link with the past and with the lives of our ancestors.

Computers have now made it possible for Frith's many thousands of images to be accessed almost instantly. The archive offers every one of us an opportunity to examine the places where we and our families have lived and worked down the years. Its images, depicting our shared past, are now bringing pleasure and enlightenment to millions around the world a century and more after his death.

For further information visit: www.francisfrith.com

INTERIOR DECORATION

Frith's photographs can be seen framed and as giant wall murals in thousands of pubs, restaurants, hotels, banks, retail stores and other public buildings throughout Britain. These provide interesting and attractive décor, generating strong local interest and acting as a powerful reminder of gentler days in our increasingly busy and frenetic world.

FRITH PRODUCTS

All Frith photographs are available as prints and posters in a variety of different sizes and styles. In the UK we also offer a range of other gift and stationery products illustrated with Frith photographs, although many of these are not available for delivery outside the UK – see our web site for more information on the products available for delivery in your country.

THE INTERNET

Over 100,000 photographs of Britain can be viewed and purchased on the Frith web site. The web site also includes memories and reminiscences contributed by our customers, who have personal knowledge of localities and of the people and properties depicted in Frith photographs. If you wish to learn more about a specific town or village you may find these reminiscences fascinating to browse. Why not add your own comments if you think they would be of interest to others? See **www.francisfrith.com**

PLEASE HELP US BRING FRITH'S PHOTOGRAPHS TO LIFE

Our authors do their best to recount the history of the places they write about. They give insights into how particular towns and villages developed, they describe the architecture of streets and buildings, and they discuss the lives of famous people who lived there. But however knowledgeable our authors are, the story they tell is necessarily incomplete.

Frith's photographs are so much more than plain historical documents. They are living proofs of the flow of human life down the generations. They show real people at real moments in history; and each of those people is the son or daughter of someone, the brother or sister, aunt or uncle, grandfather or grandmother of someone else. All of them lived, worked and played in the streets depicted in Frith's photographs.

We would be grateful if you would give us your insights into the places shown in our photographs: the streets and buildings, the shops, businesses and industries. Post your memories of life in those streets on the Frith website: what it was like growing up there, who ran the local shop and what shopping was like years ago; if your workplace is shown tell us about your working day and what the building is used for now. Read other visitors' memories and reconnect with your shared local history and heritage. With your help more and more Frith photographs can be brought to life, and vital memories preserved for posterity, and for the benefit of historians in the future.

Wherever possible, we will try to include some of your comments in future editions of our books. Moreover, if you spot errors in dates, titles or other facts, please let us know, because our archive records are not always completely accurate—they rely on 140 years of human endeavour and hand-compiled records. You can email us using the contact form on the website.

Thank you!

For further information, trade, or author enquiries
please contact us at the address below:

**The Francis Frith Collection, Oakley Business Park,
Wylye Road, Dinton, Wiltshire SP3 5EU.**

Tel: +44 (0)1722 716 376 Fax: +44 (0)1722 716 881
e-mail: sales@francisfrith.co.uk **www.francisfrith.com**